Do It To A Finish!

ORISON SWETT MARDEN

COSIMOCLASSICS

NEW YORK

Did you ever notice how much better you feel
after having done a superb piece of work,
how much more you think of yourself,
how it tones up your whole character?
What a thrill one feels when
contemplating his masterpiece…

—from "Where Only the Best Is Good Enough"

TABLE OF CONTENTS

CHAPTER ONE

THE CRIME OF CARELESSNESS

Years ago a relief lifeboat at New London sprung a leak, and while being repaired a hammer was found in the bottom that had been left there by the builders thirteen years before. From the constant motion of the boat the hammer had worn through the planking, clear down to the plating.

Not long since, it was discovered that a girl had served *twenty years* for a twenty months' sentence, in an Alabama prison, because of the mistake of a court clerk who wrote "years" instead of "months" in the record of the prisoner's sentence.

The history of the human race is full of the most horrible tragedies caused by carelessness and the inexcusable blunders of those who never formed the habit of accuracy, of thoroughness, of doing things to a finish.

Multitudes of people are hobbling around on one leg, have lost an eye or an arm, or are otherwise maimed, because dishonest workmen wrought deception into the articles they manufactured, slighted their work, covered up defects and weak places with paint and varnish.

How many have lost their lives because of dishonest work, carelessness, criminal blundering in railroad construction? Think of the tragedies caused by lied packed in car-wheels, locomotives, steamboat boilers, and engines; lies in defective rails, ties, or switches; lies in dishonest labor put into manufactured material by workmen who said it was good enough for the meager wages they got! Because people were not conscientious in their work there were flaws in the steel, which caused the rail or pillar to snap, the locomotive or other machinery to break. The steel shaft broke in mid-ocean, and the lives of a thousand passengers were jeopardized because of somebody's carelessness.

How many serious accidents have occurred because of lack of care in the casting of steel girders and all sorts of iron building material! Even before they are completed, buildings often fall and bury the workmen under their ruins, because somebody was dishonest—either employer or employee—and worked lies, deceptions, into the building.

A big mill in a manufacturing city in Massachusetts fell one day while in full operation. The ruins accidentally took fire, and one hundred and twenty-five lives were sacrificed. The disaster was the result of the grossest carelessness of the superintendent, or master-builder. Iron columns were put in that were defective in casting. They were thin as paper on one side, and as thick as a plank on the other, when they should have been true to a hairline all around. When the pressure came upon them, they were quickly broken, and botched work claimed its fearful holocaust of human lives.

Some time ago the world was startled by the collapse of a great bridge in Canada, which caused the loss of many precious lives and millions of dollars in property. "On August 29 last," said the newspaper reports of the disaster, "twenty thousand tons of steel, which had in the course of several years been laboriously worked into the south arm of a great cantilever bridge over the St. Lawrence River at Quebec, suddenly crumpled up like so much cardboard and fell into the river, carrying with it nearly a hundred human beings. Of these over seventy were crushed to death or drowned. Besides this terrible loss of life the disaster must have cost the builders of the bridge millions of dollars—all wiped out of existence in a few seconds."

Before the investigating committee appointed by the Canadian government to inquire into the matter, Mr. Theodore Cooper, the consulting engineer of the bridge, an expert in his profession, gave the following testimony:

"I believe if prompt action had been taken to protect chord nine west from further deflection, which could have been done by the employment of three hours' work and one hundred dollars' worth of timber and bolts, the defects and deficiencies which we now recognize in the compression chords and members could, at a later date, have been corrected, and the bridge could have been made perfectly safe and sufficient for its intended purpose."

Here was a double crime: carelessness or negligence on the part of the constructing engineers or some of those employed in building the bridge in the first instance, which made the collapse at all possible; in the second place, criminal carelessness on the part of those responsible for the condition of the bridge, who might have prevented the

3

fatal accident by the exercise of a little ordinary care and intelligence, the expenditure of a few hours' work and a hundred dollars' worth of material!

The majority of railroad wrecks, of disasters on land and sea, which cause so much misery and cost so many lives, are the result of carelessness, thoughtlessness, or half-done, botched, blundering work. They are the evil fruit of the low ideals of slovenly, careless, indifferent workers.

Everywhere over this broad earth we see the tragic results of botched work. Wooden legs, armless sleeves, numberless graves, father-less and motherless homes every-where speak of somebody's carelessness, somebody's blunders, somebody's habit of inaccuracy.

The worst crimes are not punishable by law. Careless-ness, slipshodness, lack of thoroughness, are crimes against self, against humanity, that often do more harm than the crimes that make the perpetrator an outcast from society. Where a tiny flaw or the slightest defect may cost a precious life, carelessness is as much a crime as deliberate criminality.

If everybody put his conscience into his work, did it to a complete finish, it would not only reduce the loss of human life, the mangling and maiming of men and women, to a fraction of what it is at present, but it would also give us a higher quality of manhood and womanhood.

It takes honest work to make an honest character. The habit of doing poor, slovenly work will, after a while, make the worker dishonest in other things. The man who habitually slights his work slights his character. Botched work makes a botched life. Our work is a part of us. Every botched job you let go through your hands diminishes your competence, your efficiency, your ability to do good work. It is an offence against your self-respect, an insult to your highest ideal. Every inferior piece of work you do is an enemy, which pulls you down, keeps you from getting on.

CHAPTER TWO

THE RELATION OF WORK TO CHARACTER

Nothing kills ambition or lowers the life standard quicker than familiarity with inferiority—that which is cheap, the "cheap John" method of doing things. We unconsciously become like that with which we are habitually associated. It becomes part of us, and the habit of doing things in an inferior, slovenly way weaves its fatal defects into the very texture of the character and becomes part of the life-web.

Most young people think too much of quantity, and too little of quality in their work. They try to do too much, and do not do it well. They do not realize that the education, the comfort, the satisfaction, the general improvement, and bracing up of the whole man that comes from doing one thing absolutely right, from putting the trademark of one's character on it, far outweighs the value that attaches to the doing of a thousand botched or slipshod jobs.

We are so constituted that the quality which we put into our life-work affects everything else in our lives, and tends to bring our whole conduct to the same level. The entire person takes on the characteristics of one's usual way of doing things. The habit of precision and accuracy strengthens the mentality, improves the whole character.

On the contrary, doing things in a loose-jointed, slipshod, careless manner deteriorates the whole mentality, demoralizes the mental processes, and pulls down the whole life.

Every half-done or slovenly job that goes out of your hands leaves its trace of demoralization behind, takes a bit from your self-respect. After slighting your work, after doing a poor job, you are not quite the same man you were before. You are not so likely to try to keep up the quality of your work, not so likely to regard your word as sacred as before. You incapacitate yourself for doing your best in proportion to the number of times you allow yourself to do inferior, slipshod work.

The mental and moral effect of half doing, or carelessly doing things; its power to drag down, to demoralize, can hardly be estimated because the processes are so gradual, so subtle. No one can respect he who habitually botches his work, and when self-respect drops, confidence goes with it; and when confidence and self-respect have gone, excellence is impossible.

It is astonishing how completely a slovenly habit will gradually, insidiously fasten itself upon the individual and so change his whole mental attitude as to thwart absolutely his life-purpose, even when he may think he is doing his best to carry it out.

7

I know a man who was extremely ambitious to do something very distinctive and who had the ability to do it. When he started on his career he was very exact and painstaking. He demanded the best of himself—would not accept his second-best in anything. The thought of slighting his work was painful to him, but his mental processes have so deteriorated, and he has become so demoralized by the habit, which, after a while, grew upon him, of accepting his second-best, that he does it now without a protest, seemingly without being conscious of it. He is today doing quite ordinary things, without apparent mortification or sense of humiliation, and the tragedy of it all is, *he does not know why he has failed!*

One's ambition and ideals need constant watching and cultivation in order to keep the standards up. Many people are so constituted that their ambition wanes and their ideals drop when they are alone, or with careless, indifferent people. They require the constant assistance, suggestion, prodding, or example of others to keep them up to standard.

I recall a once prominent man who, until the death of his wife, had very high ideals and a lofty aim; a man who was extremely painstaking and careful in everything, who would never accept anything from himself but the best he was capable of, but who, when he lives alone, gradually dropped his lofty standards, neglected his appearance, and grew so slovenly in his personal habits, that he became really repulsive, and yet he was, apparently, absolutely unconscious of the insidious change.

How quickly a youth of high ideals, who has been well trained in thoroughness, often deteriorates when he leaves home and goes to work for an employer with inferior ideals and slipshod methods!

The introduction of inferiority into our work is like introducing subtle poison into the system. It paralyzes the normal functions. Inferiority is an infection, which, like leaven, affects the entire system. It dulls ideals, palsies the aspiring faculty, stupefies the ambition, and causes deterioration all along the line.

The human mechanism is so constituted that whatever goes wrong in one part affects the whole structure. There is a very intimate relation between the quality of the work and the quality of the character. Did you ever notice the rapid decline in a young man's character when he began to slight his work, to shirk, to slip in rotten hours, rotten service?

If you should ask the inmates of our penitentiaries what had caused their ruin, many of them could trace the first signs of deterioration to shirking, clipping their hours, deceiving their employers—to indifferent, dishonest work.

We were made to be honest. Honesty is our normal expression, and any departure from it demoralizes and taints the whole character. Honest means integrity in everything. It not only means reliability in your word, but also carefulness, accuracy, honesty in your work. It does not mean that if only you will not lie with your lips you may lie and defraud in the quality of your work. Honesty means wholeness, completeness; it means truth in everything—in deed and in word. Merely not to steal another's money or goods is not all there is to honesty. You must not steal another's time, you must not steal his goods or ruin his property by half finishing or botching your work, by blundering through carelessness or indifference. Your contract with your employer means that you will give him your best, and not your second-best.

Aside from the question of honesty, of its effect on yourself, you can't afford to give the dregs of yourself and your efforts to the man who hires you to do your best, for it will bring only dregs back to you.

"What a food you are," said one workman to another, "to take so much pains with that job, when you don't get much pay for it. 'Get the most money for the least work,' is my rule, and I get twice as much money as you do."

"That may be," replied the other, "but I shall like myself better, I shall think more of myself, and that is more important to me than money."

You will like yourself better when you have the approval of your conscience. That will be worth more to you than any amount of money you can pocket through fraudulent, skimped, or botched work. Nothing else can give you the glow of satisfaction, the electric thrill and uplift, which come from a superbly done job. Perfect work harmonizes with the very principles of our being, because we were made for perfection. It fits our very natures.

CHAPTER THREE

BLUNDERS THAT COST A MILLION DOLLARS A DAY

Someone has said: "It is a race between negligence and ignorance as to which can make the more trouble."

Many a young man is being kept down by what probably seems a small thing to him—negligence, lack of accuracy. He never quite finishes anything he undertakes; he cannot be depended upon to do anything quite right; his work always needs looking over by someone else. Hundreds of clerks and bookkeepers are getting small salaries in poor positions today because they have never learned to do things absolutely right.

A prominent businessman says that the carelessness, inaccuracy, and blundering of employees cost Chicago one million dollars a day. The manager of a large Chicago house says that he has to station pickets here and there through the establishment in order to neutralize the evils of inaccuracy and the blundering habit. One of John

Wanamaker's partners says that unnecessary blunders and mistakes cost that firm twenty-five thousand dollars a year. The dead letter department of the Post Office in Washington received in one-year seven million pieces of undelivered mail. Of these more than eighty thousand bore no address whatsoever. A great many of them were from business houses. Are the clerks responsible for this carelessness likely to win promotion?

Many an employee who would be shocked at the thought of telling his employer a lie with his lips is lying every day in the quality of his work, in his dishonest service, in the rotten hours he is slipping into it, in shirking, in his indifference to his employer's interests. It is just as dishonest to express it with the lips, yet I have known office boys, who could not be induced to tell their employer a direct lie, to steal his time when on an errand, to hide away during working hours to smoke a cigarette or take a nap, not realizing, perhaps, that lies can be acted as well as told and that acting a lie may be even worse than telling one.

Every man who perverts in any way the normal expression of himself, which is honesty, integrity, wholeness, is dishonest, untruthful; and every faculty which is not normally and healthfully used deteriorates. The man who botches his work, who lies or cheats in the goods he sells or manufactures, who uses weak, poor, rotten or inferior material where it may be covered up with paint and varnish is dishonest with himself as well as with his fellow men, and must pay the price in loss of self-respect, loss of character, of standing in his community.

Yet on every side we see all sorts of things selling for a song because the maker put no character, no thought into them. Articles of clothing that look stylish and attractive when first worn, very quickly get out of shape, and hang and look like old, much-worn garments. Buttons fly off, seams give way at the slightest strain, dropped stitches are everywhere in evidence, and often the entire article goes to pieces before it is worn half a dozen times. Many people never think of putting on a ready-made garment until the buttons are sewn on again, and often the seams re-stitched.

Everywhere we see furniture, which looks all right, but in reality is full of blemishes and weaknesses, covered up with paint and varnish. Glue starts at joints, chairs and bedsteads break down at the slightest provocation, castors come off, handles pull out, and many things "go to pieces" altogether, even while practically new.

I have known a buggy to collapse completely before it had been in use three months. The varnish and paint peeled off and revealed spongy spokes, knotted wood, open joints and all sorts of slovenly work.

"Made to sell, not for service," would be a good label for the great mass of manufactured articles in our markets today.

If the half-made, dishonest, botched manufactured articles could only come out from their disguises, and speak the truth, they would say, "Don't buy me, you poor laboring people. I was made only to sell, not for service. Not even rich people could afford such extravagance. I shall go all to pieces before I am half worn out."

The cheap, shoddy articles of clothing would say, "Don't buy me. My buttons will fly off, and my seams rip the first time you wear me. I shall very quickly get out of shape, and the first time I get wet the shoddy in me will reveal my deception."

The painted and varnished shams would say, "Don't judge me by my appearance. There are lots of lies under my cover, lies of rotten, spongy, cross-grained, knotty wood, and gaping joints, covered up by a coat of putty, paint, and varnish. I am only for show, not for use."

It is difficult to find anything that is well and honestly made, that has character, individuality and thoroughness wrought into it. Most things are just thrown together. This slipshod, dishonest manufacturing is so general that concerns which turn out products based upon honesty and truth often win for themselves a worldwide reputation and command the highest prices.

Probably not a woman in America but would prefer to receive a present of jewelry or silverware from Tiffany's to one from any other house. Why? Because the name Tiffany is packed full of character, because it has a reputation which it has taken nearly a century to build up; the name is synonymous with reliability, cleanness, fairness. People who trade at Tiffany's know that whether they purchase personally or by mail, they are not going to be swindled. They know that no lies, no botched, half-made or dishonest articles are sold in that house.

There is no other advertisement like a good reputation. Some of the world's greatest manufacturers have regarded their reputation as their most precious possession, and under no circumstances would they allow their names to be put on an imperfect article. Vast sums of money are often paid for the use of a name, because of its great reputation for integrity and square dealing. There are concerns in New York whose names as a trademark would probably sell for a million dollars or more, because they are synonymous with integrity. They embody the public confidence.

There was a time when the names of Graham and Tampion on timepieces were guarantees of the most exquisite workmanship and of unquestioned integrity. Strangers from any part of the world could send their purchase money and order goods from those manufacturers without a doubt that they would be squarely dealt with.

Graham made the Greenwich Observatory clock, which furnishes the standard time to the nations, and still requires regulating only once in fifteen months.

Tampion and Graham lie in Westminster Abbey because of the accuracy of their work—because they refused to manufacture and sell lies.

CHAPTER FOUR

THE DIFFERENCE BETWEEN ARTIST AND ARTISAN

When you finish a thing you ought to be able to say to yourself: "There, I am willing to stand for that piece of work. It is not pretty well done; it is done as well as I can do it; done to a complete finish. I will stand for that. I am willing to be judged by it."

Never be satisfied with "fairly good," "pretty good," "good enough." Accept nothing short of your best. Put such a quality into your work that anyone who comes across anything you have ever done will see character in it, individuality in it, your trademark of superiority upon it. Your reputation is at stake in everything you do, and your reputation is your capital. You cannot afford to do a poor job, to let botched work or anything that is inferior go out of your hands. Every bit of your work, no matter how unimportant or trivial it may seem, should bear your trademark of excellence; you should regard every task that

16

goes through your hands, every piece of work you touch, as Tampion regarded every watch that went out of his shop. It must be the very best you can do, the best that human skill can produce.

It is just the little difference between the good and the best that makes the difference between the artist and the artisan. It is just the little touches after the average man would quit that make the master's fame.

Regard your work as Stradivarius regarded his violins, which he "made for eternity," and not one of which was ever known to come to pieces or break. When a piece of work leaves your hand it should bear your recommendation, the hallmark of your character.

Stradivarius did not need any patent on his violins, for no other violin maker would pay such a price for excellence as he paid; would take such pains to put his stamp of superiority upon his instruments. He was determined from the outset to make his name on a violin worth something, to make it a trademark, which would protect the instrument the world over. His reputation was his patent; he needed no other. Every "Stradivarius" now in existence is worth from three to ten thousand dollars, or several times its weight in gold.

Think of the value such a reputation for thoroughness as that of Stradivarius or Tampion, such a passion to give quality to your work, would give you! There is nothing like being enamored of accuracy, being grounded in thoroughness as a life-principle, of always striving for excellence.

No other characteristic makes such a strong impression upon an employer as the habit of painstaking, carefulness, accuracy. He knows that if a youth puts his conscience into his work from principle, not from the standpoint of salary or what he can get for it, but because there is something in him which refuses to accept anything from himself but the best, that he is honest and made of good material.

I have known many instances where advancement hinged upon the little over plus of interest, of painstaking an employee put into his work, on his doing a little better than was expected of him. Employers are no fools. They do not say all they think, but they detect very quickly the earmarks of superiority. They keep their eye on the employee who has the stamp of excellence upon him, who takes pains with his work, who does it to a finish. They know he has a future.

John D. Rockefeller, Jr., says that the "secret of success is to do the common duty uncommonly well." The majority of young people do not see that the steps, which lead to the position above them are constructed, little by little, by the faithful performance of the common, humble, everyday duties of the position they are now filling. The thing, which you are now doing will unlock or bar the door to promotion.

Many employees are looking for some great thing to happen that will give them an opportunity to show their mettle. "What an there be," they say to themselves, "in this dry routine, in doing these common, ordinary things, to help me along?" But it is the youth who sees a great opportunity hidden in just these simple services, who sees a very uncommon chance in a common situation, a humble position, who gets on in the world. It is doing things a little better than those about you do them; being a little neater, a little quicker, a little more accurate, a little more observant;

it is ingenuity in finding new and more progressive ways of doing old things; it is being a little more polite, a little more obliging, a little more tactful, a little more cheerful, optimistic, a little more energetic, helpful, than those about you that attracts the attention of your employer and other employers also.

Many a boy is marked for a higher position by his employer long before he is aware of it himself. It may be months, or it may be a year before the opening comes, but when it does come the one who has appreciated the infinite difference between "good" and "better," between "fairly good" and "excellent," between what others call "good" and the best that can be done, will be likely to get the place.

One of the earmarks of success is the desire to do things to a finish; to be as particular in doing small things as in doing big things. The boy who is going to succeed is not satisfied to do anything "pretty well," or to leave things half finished. Nothing but completion to perfection will satisfy the demand in him for the best. It is those who have this imperative demand for the best in their natures, and who will accept nothing short of it, that hold the banners of progress, that set the standards, the ideals, for others.

One of the most successful men I know stamped his individuality upon everybody who knew him by this constant desire for the highest and the best in everything. No one could induce him to half do a thing, or to accept an inferior article when a better was within his reach. Whether it was the quality and the style of his clothing, or of anything that he bought, he would allow nothing about him which was not the best obtainable. Even when poor and trying to get a start for himself, when others patronized cheap restaurants and obtained rooms in cheap localities, he would have none of these things.

He believed that his success depended largely upon following high ideals, upon keeping himself up to quality, upon his making a good impression, and he would not have anything to do with cheap or shoddy things. He shrank from inferiority, and avoided it as he would poison, believing that it would taint his ideals, smirch his ambition, and lower his standards. No cheap, ill-printed books; no cheap, shoddy clothing; no cheap, poverty-stricken rooms for him. He had to have the best or nothing.

His acquaintances thought that it was foolish and ruinous for him, when trying to establish himself in his profession, to spend his entire income in keeping up appearances or trying to keep in touch with the best people. He always considered that it was worth much, however, to be thrown with people of culture and refinement, people of means, because he expected they would be his patrons later in life. He believed that social success was imperative to his professional success, and for that reason, he regarded his acquaintance with the better classes as of inestimable value. His subsequent career certainly seemed to vindicate his methods. Although he had a hard struggle at first, he has attained great distinction, and has been a marvel to his schoolmates and those who knew him in early life as a poor boy, and who laughed at the lofty standard, which he set for himself.

The main value of this man's career is in its suggestion that we should allow nothing to enter the life that will deteriorate our ideals or lower our standard of quality. It teaches that keeping with the beset, doing our best, insisting upon the best everywhere and always, will have a marked influence in elevating the life to the standard adopted.

If there is that in your nature, which demands the best and will take nothing less; if you insist on keeping up your standards in everything you do, you will achieve distinction in some line, provided you have the persistence and determination to follow your ideal.

But if you are satisfied with the cheap and shoddy, the botched and slovenly, if you are not particular about quality in your work, or in your environment, or in your personal habits, then you must expect to take second place, to fall back to the rear of the procession.

People who have accomplished work worthwhile have had a very high sense of the way to do things. They have not been content with mediocrity. They have not confined themselves to the beaten tracks; they have never been satisfied to do things just as others do them, but always a little better. They always pushed things that came to their hands a little higher up, a little farther on. It is this little higher up, this little farther on, that counts in the quality of life's work. It is the constant effort to be first-class in everything one attempts that conquers the heights of excellence.

CHAPTER FIVE

SECOND-CLASS MEN

It is said that Daniel Webster made the best chowder in his state on the principle that he would not be second-class in anything. This is a good resolution with which to start out in your career; never to be second-class in anything. No matter what you do, try to do it as well as it can be done. Have nothing to do with the inferior. Do your best in everything; deal with the best; choose the best; live up to your best. Don't be second-class in anything.

You can hardly imagine a boy saying: "I am going to be a second-class man. I don't want to be first-class and get the good jobs, the high pay. Second-class jobs are good enough for me." Such a boy would be regarded as lacking in good sense, if not in sanity. Yet this, in effect, is what boys everywhere are expressing, in their studies, their work, their conduct, in everything they do. In not trying to do their best, they are training for mediocrity, or complete failure. You can become a second-class man, simply by not trying to be a first-class one. Thousands do that all the time so that second-class men are a drug in the market.

Everywhere we see those mediocre or second-class men—perpetual clerks who will never get away from the yardstick; mechanics who will never be anything but bunglers, all sorts of people who will never rise above mediocrity, who will always fill very ordinary positions because they do not take pains, do not put conscience into their work, do not try to be first-class.

Aside from the lack of desire or effort to be first-class, there are other things that help to make second-class men. Dissipation, bad habits, neglect of health, failure to get an education, all make second-class men. A man weakened by dissipation, whose understanding has been dulled, whose growth has been stunted by self-indulgences, is a second-class man, if, indeed, he is not third-class. A man who, through his amusements in his hours of leisure, exhausts his strength and vitality, vitiates his blood, wears his nerves till his limbs tremble like leaves in the wind, is only half a man, and could in no sense be called first-class.

Everybody knows the things that make for second-class characteristics. Boys imitate older boys and smoke cigarettes in order to be "smart." Then they keep on smoking because they have created an appetite as unnatural as it is harmful. Men get drunk for all sorts of reasons; but, whatever the reason, they cannot remain first-class men and drink. Dissipation in other forms is pursued because of pleasures to be derived, but the surest consequence is that of becoming second-class, below the standard of the best men for any purpose.

Every fault you allow to become a habit, to get control over you, helps to make you second-class, and puts you at a disadvantage in the race for honor, position, wealth, and happiness. Carelessness as to health fills the ranks of the inferior. The submerged classes that the economists talk about are those that are below the high-water mark of the best manhood and womanhood. Sometimes they are second-rate or third-rate people because those who are responsible for their being and their care during their minor years were so before them, but more and more is it becoming one's own fault if, all through life, he remains second-class. Education of some sort, and even a pretty good sort, is possible to practically everyone in our land. Failure to get the best education available, whether it be in books or in business training, is sure to relegate one to the ranks of the second-class.

It is in every man to be first-class in something, if he will. Only himself can hold him back. There is no excuse for incompetence in this age of opportunity; no excuse for being second-class when it is possible to be first-class, and when first-class is in demand everywhere.

Second-class things are wanted only when first-class can't be had. You wear first-class clothes if you can pay for them, eat first-class butter, first-class meat, and first-class bread, or, if you don't, you wish you could. Second-class men are no more wanted than any other second-class commodity. They are taken and used when the better article is scarce or is too high-priced for the occasion. For work that really amounts to anything, first-class men are wanted. If you make yourself first-class in anything, no matter what your condition or circumstances, no matter what your race or color, you will be in demand. If you are a king in your calling, no matter how humble it may be, nothing can keep you from success.

Some years ago a young man was graduated from Tuskegee who had taken the course in dairying. A friend of the institution, being called upon to recommend a suitable manager to a firm of white men about to open a dairy, named this young man, concerning the color of whose skin nothing was said. When the black man presented himself, the astonishment was complete, and the president of the company began to talk about the man's color. The young man reminded the president that he had come to talk about the making of butter, and so the conversation oscillated from butter to color, and from color to butter, until finally it was agreed that the young man should have a trial; but there was no decision to retain a man of his complexion until returns came from his first shipment of butter to New York City. When these were to the effect that the butter prepared by him had brought one cent a pound more than any butter that had been shipped before from the community, he became about half white; and when the returns from the second or third shipment showed that the butter manufactured by him realized something over two cents a pound more than any butter ever before shipped from that point, he became entirely white, so far as the eyes of that firm were concerned. It is said that the fact that this young man was able to develop the productive industry of that community by two cents a pound on butter has proved the only successful bleaching device that has been discovered there.

The world does not demand that you be a physician, a lawyer, a farmer, or a merchant; but it does demand that whatever you do undertake, you will do it right, will do it with all your might and with all the ability you possess. It demands that you be a master in your line.

CHAPTER SIX

THOROUGHNESS: THE HANDMAID OF GENIUS

When Daniel Webster, who had the best brain of his time, was asked to make a speech on some question at the close of a Congressional session, he replied: "I never allow myself to speak on any subject until I have made it my own. I haven't time to do that in this case, hence, I must refuse to speak on the subject."

Mr. Webster once made a very brilliant speech (which was supposed at the time to be impromptu) upon the occasion of the presentation to him of a book by the Phi Beta Kappa society of Harvard. After he had left, however, it was found that he had forgotten to take the book with him, and the carefully prepared speech was discovered inside it.

Dickens would never consent to read before an audience until he had thoroughly prepared his selection. It was his practice to read a piece once a day for six months before giving it in public.

Balzac, the great French novelist, sometimes worked a week on a single page, and yet many a modern mushroom writer wonders where Balzac's fame comes from.

Macready, when playing before scant audiences in country theatres in England, Ireland, and Scotland, always played as if he were before the most brilliant audiences in the great metropolises of the world. "Before the most meager audiences ever assembled," he once said, "it has been my invariable practice to strive my best, using the opportunity as a lesson; and I am conscious of having derived great benefit from the rule. I used to call it acting to myself."

Thoroughness characterizes all successful men. Genius is the art of taking infinite pains. The trouble with many Americans is that they seem to think they can put any sort of poor, slipshod, half-done work into their careers and get first-class products. They do not realize that all great achievement has been characterized by extreme care, infinite painstaking, even to the minutest detail. No youth can ever hope to accomplish much who does not have thoroughness and accuracy indelibly fixed in his life-habit. Slipshodness, inaccuracy, the habit of half doing things, would ruin the career of a youth with a Napoleon's mind.

If we were to examine a list of the men who have left their mark on the world, we should find that, as a rule, it is not composed of those who were brilliant in youth, or who gave great promise at the outset of their careers, but rather of the plodding young men who, if they have not dazzled by their brilliancy, have had the power of a day's work in them, who could stay by a task until it was done, and well done; who have had grit, persistence, common sense, and honesty.

It is the steady exercise of these ordinary, homely virtues, united with average ability, rather than a deceptive display of more showy qualities in youth, that enables a man to achieve greatly and honorably. So, if we were to attempt to make a forecast of the successful men of the future, we should not look for them among the ranks of the "smart" boys, those who think they "know it all" and are anxious to win by a short route.

The thorough boys are the boys that are heard from, and usually from posts far higher up than those filled by the boys who were too "smart" to be thorough. One such boy is Elihu Root, now United States Senator. When he was a boy in the grammar school at Clinton, New York, he made up his mind that anything he had to study he would keep at until he mastered it. Although not considered one of the "bright" boys of the school, his teacher soon found that when Elihu professed to know anything he knew it through and through. He was fond of hard problems requiring application and patience. Sometimes the other boys called him a plodder, but Elihu would only smile pleasantly, for he knew what he was about. On winter evenings, while the other boys were out skating, Elihu frequently remained in his room with his arithmetic or algebra. Mr. Root recently said that if his close application to problems in his boyhood did nothing else for him, it made him careful about jumping at conclusions. To every problem there was only one answer, and patience was the price to be paid for it. Carrying the principle of "doing everything to a finish" into the law, he became one of the most noted members of the New York bar, entrusted with vast interests, and then a member of the President's cabinet.

William Ellery Channing, the great New England divine, who in his youth was hardly able to buy the clothes he needed, had a passion for self-improvement. "I wanted to make the most of myself," he says; "I was not satisfied with knowing things superficially and by halves, but tried to get comprehensive views of what I studied."

The quality, which, more than any other, has helped to raise the German people to their present commanding position in the world, is their thoroughness. Germans do not half do things. The slipshod methods, which characterize many Americans are practically unknown to the Germans, who are patient in investigation and thorough down to the smallest details.

The Teutonic mind is orderly and methodical; it makes haste slowly by doing everything completely, as well as it can be done.

This quality of doing everything to a finish is giving young Germans a great advantage over both English and American youths. Every employer is looking for thoroughness, and German employees, owing to their preeminence in this respect, the superiority of their training, and the completeness of their preparation for business, are in great demand today in England, especially in banks and large mercantile houses.

It is an exception to find an English-speaking youth who can use any language but his own, whereas the majority of young Germans can speak and write several languages. They go to France and England and serve without pay in order to learn French and English. If you are a merchant and have any transactions with French houses, you will notice that, except in rare instances, Frenchmen correspond with you in their mother tongue. This is not the case with Germans. On account of their knowledge of languages, they are able to carry on their correspondence in the vernacular of the country with which they trade. Owing to the rapid increase in foreign trade in countries like England and America, for example, this gives them a great advantage.

Unfortunately the average American youth thinks that he can succeed with any kind of preparation. He believes that his "smartness" will take the place of broad and firm foundations, and will ultimately "win out" for him. This is a fatal mistake; for, even with the American's native adaptability to varying conditions, which is, undoubtedly, a strong point in his favor, the German's thorough preparation and ability to master details gives him a great advantage at the outset of his career.

As a rule, a German who expects to engage in business takes a four years' course in some commercial school, and after graduation serves three years' apprenticeship, without pay, to his chosen business.

Thoroughness and reliability, the German's characteristics, are increasing the power of Germany throughout the civilized world.

Our great lack is want of thoroughness. How seldom you find a young man or woman who is willing to prepare for his life work. A little education is all they want, a little smattering of books, and then they are ready for business.

Not long ago a professor in one of our universities had a letter from a young woman in the West, asking him if he did not think she could teach elocution, if she could come to the university and take twelve lessons!

In an examination in primary schools in Massachu-setts, out of eleven hundred and twenty-two pupils who used the word "too," eight hundred and fifty-nine spelled it incorrectly. Twenty-seven ways of spelling "Cyrus" were used by advanced scholars.

They had fifty ways of spelling the word "which." The word "whose" was spelled in more than a hundred ways. "School" was spelled in two hundred ways.

The following examples of spelling were taken from the examination papers of candidates for Harvard College: "Duells, jelosie, opposit, repetedly, ficle, beveradge, insted, preasant, wating, superceeded, conspiritors, avaritious, undoubtibly, peece, couardise, origen, differculty, proc-lamed, loose for 'lose,' champaign for 'champagne,' finnish, Rip Van Rincle, Adison and Adderson, Queene Ann, Hen-ery, Harries for 'Harry's.'"

The shifts to cover up ignorance, and "the constant trembling lest some blunder should expose one's empti-ness," are pitiable. Shortcuts and abridged methods are the demand of the hour.

"Can't wait," "haven't time to be thorough," is charac-teristic of our country, and is written on everything—on commerce, on schools, on society, on churches. We can't wait for a high school, seminary, or college education. The boy can't wait to become a youth, nor the youth to become a man. Young men rush into business with no great reserve of education or drill; or course; they do poor, feverish work, and break down in middle life, while many die of old age in the forties.

Perhaps there is no other country in the world where so much poor work is done as in America. Half-trained medical students perform bungling operations, and butcher their patients, because they are not willing to take time for thorough preparation. Half-trained lawyers stumble through their cases, and make their clients pay for experience, which the law school should have given. Half-trained clergymen bungle away in the pulpit, and disgust their intelligent and cultured parishioners. Many an American youth is willing to stumble through life half prepared for his work, and then blame society because he is a failure. Nature works for centuries to perfect a rose or a fruit, but an American youth is ready to try a difficult case in court after a few months' desultory law reading, or to undertake a critical operation upon which a precious life depends after listening to two or three courses of medical lectures.

CHAPTER SEVEN

THAT FATAL "ALMOST"

A young man, armed with letters of introduction from prominent men, one day presented himself before Chief Engineer Parsons, of the Rapid Transit Commission of New York as a candidate for a position. "What can you do? Have you any specialty?" asked Mr. Parsons. "I can do almost anything," answered the young man. "Well," remarked the Chief Engineer, rising to end the interview, "I have no use for anyone who can 'almost' do anything. I prefer someone who can actually do one thing thoroughly."

There is a great crowd of human beings just outside the door of proficiency. They can half do a great many things, but can't do any one thing well, to a finish. They have acquisitions, which remain permanently unavailable because they were not carried quite to the point of skill; they stopped just short of efficiency. How many people almost know a language or two, which they can neither write nor speak; a science or two, whose elements they have not fully mastered; an art or two, which they cannot practice with satisfaction or profit!

Everywhere we meet people who are almost successful. Here is a man who is almost a lawyer, but not quite; here is another who is almost a physician, but is neither a good druggist, a good surgeon, nor a good dispenser. Another man is almost a clergyman, or about halfway between a farmer, or a tradesman, and a clergyman. Another is almost a teacher, but not quite competent to take charge of a school or an academy. In every country there are men and women who are almost something, but just a little short of it.

If these people undertake anything, they never quite finish it; they never quite complete their courses at school; they never quite learn a trade or profession. They always manage to stop just short of success.

In thousands of American homes, lying, perhaps, in the attic, woodshed, or workshop, are scores of ingenious, labor-saving devices, or inventions, which, if carried a step further and patented, would not only give those who originated them a competence for life, but would enrich the civilization of the world. But the thinkers get discouraged or tired, or lack persistency, the habit of carrying things to completion; and so the half-developed machinery, the embryo invention, has never come to light, and the time spent upon it has been lost, perhaps worse than lost, because the lesson of perseverance, persistency, thoroughness was not learned.

The Patent Office at Washington contains hundreds—yes, thousands—of inventions which are useless simply because they are not quite practical, because the men who started them lacked the staying quality, the education, or the ability necessary to carry them to the point of practicability. Edison has been shrewd enough to carry many of these half-finished inventions to useful application and commercial success.

The world is full of half-finished work—failures, which require only a little more persistence, a little finer mechanical training, a little better education, to make them useful to civilization. Would that we had a thousand Edisons to pick up all such dropped cords or threads, half-finished inventions, abortive attempts and discoveries, which have stopped just this side of practicability! What a blessing to civilization are men who can do things to a finish, who complete what they undertake, who leave nothing half done! Think what a loss it would be if such men as Edison and Bell had not come to the front and carried to a successful termination the half-finished work of others!

"Almost" is a dangerous word. It has tripped up many a man who might have been successful if he had formed the habit of painstaking thoroughness in youth, the habit of doing everything he undertook to a finish.

There are multitudes of people today plodding along in mediocrity, many of whom lay down right in sigh of their goal, just because they were satisfied when young with "almost" doing things; "almost" learning their lessons; "almost" finishing the tasks they were given to do. Like the boy who was sent after the sheep that had strayed away from the flock but who returned without them, and in answer to his father's query if he had found the sheep, said, "Yes, almost, father," they never seemed to realize the gulf that separates "almost" from "to a finish."

CHAPTER EIGHT

WHAT EVERY EMPLOYER IS LOOKING FOR

A successful manufacturer says: "If you make a good pin, you will earn more money than if you make a bad steam engine." "If a man can write a better book, preach a better sermon, or make a better mousetrap than his neighbor," says Emerson, "though he build his house in the woods, the world will make a path to his door."

Make it a life-rule to give your best to whatever passes through your hands. Stamp it with your manhood. Let superiority be your trademark, let it characterize everything you touch. This is what every employer is looking for. It indicates the best kind of brain; it is the best substitute for genius; it is better capital than cash; it is a better promoter than friends, or "pulls" with the influential.

Never allow yourself to dwell too much upon what you are getting for your work. You have something of infinitely greater importance, greater value, at stake. Your honor, your whole career, your future success, will be affected by the way you do your work, by the conscience or lack of it which you put into your job.

A young woman working on a newspaper said she did not try to do her best because she did not get much pay. This doing poor work because it does not pay much is just what keeps thousands of people from getting on in the world. Work is a question of character, not of remuneration. One has no right to demoralize his own character by doing slovenly or botched work simply because he is not paid much. The employee has something at stake besides his salary. Character, manhood and womanhood are at stake, compared with which salary is nothing.

Judge M——, a well-known jurist, says that he once employed a young man to mend a fence, and told him to use rough, un-planed boards, not to try to make a neat job, because he would pay him only a dollar and a half.

Later the judge found the man carefully planing the boards and doing a very fine job. Supposing that he would try to collect much more than a dollar and a half, he ordered him to nail the boards on the fence, rough, as they were, and passed on. The young man paid no attention to the order. He did the best job he could. When the judge returned, he was angry, and said to him, "I told you this fence was to be covered with vines. I don't care how it looks." "But I do," said the carpenter. "How much do you charge?" asked the judge. "A dollar and a half." "Why did you spend all that labor and pains, if not for money?" "For the job, sir." "Nobody would have seen the poor work on it." "But I should have known it was there," the young man replied. Ten years afterward the judge had the awarding of a contract for several large public buildings. "Among the bidders," he said, "I recognized my man of the fence. I gave him the contract, and it has made a rich man of him."

If you put your conscience into your work, no matter how poorly you are paid, the fruits of it will come back to you some time in some way.

No matter how meager your salary, you cannot, on your own account, afford to let work go out of your hands without your unqualified endorsement.

The job which goes out of your hands should mean that there is nothing slovenly or slipshod about it. If you have made a suit of clothes, it should mean that the seams will not part, or the buttons fly off, on the least strain; if a piece of furniture, it should mean that it is not glued where it should be dovetailed, that you have not tried to cover up weak, spongy, defective wood, where strength is necessary, with pain or varnish, or filled gaping joints with putty.

In short, everything you do is a part of your career. If any work that goes out of your hands is skimped, shirked, bungled, or botched, your character will suffer. If you work is badly done; if it goes to pieces; if there is shoddy or sham in it; if there is dishonesty in it, there is shoddy, sham, dishonesty in your character. We are all of a piece. We cannot have an honest character, a complete, untarnished career, when we are constantly slipping rotten hours, defective material and slipshod service into our work.

The man who has dealt in shams and inferiority, who has botched his work all his life, must be conscious that he has not been a real man; he cannot help feeling that his career has been a botched one.

To spend a life buying and selling lies, dealing in cheap, shoddy shams, or botching one's work, is demoralizing to every element of nobility.

No matter what the contract for your job specifies, no matter if you only get paid for doing a poor job, you cannot afford to do a poor job, or you will cheapen yourself. You will tend toward the habit of inferiority, which is fatal.

Beecher said he was never quite the same man again after reading Ruskin. You are never quite the same again after doing a poor job, after botching your work. You cannot be just to yourself and unjust to the man you are working for in the quality of your work, for, if you slight your work, you not only strike a fatal blow at your efficiency, but also smirch your character. If you would be a full man, a complete man, a just man, you must be honest to the core in the quality of your work.

CHAPTER NINE

"WHERE ONLY THE BEST IS GOOD ENOUGH"

No one can be really happy who does not believe in his own honesty, does not believe he is trying hard to do right, to be just, clean, and honest.

We are so constituted that every departure from the right, from principle, makes us unhappy, causes loss of self-respect.

Every time we obey the inward law of doing right we hear an inward approval, the amen of the soul, and a protest or condemnation every time we disobey it.

Did you ever notice how much better you feel after having done a superb piece of work, how much more you think of yourself, how it tones up your whole character? What a thrill one feels when contemplating his masterpiece, the work into which he has put the very best that was in him, the very best of which he was capable! This all comes from obeying the natural law within us to do things right, as they should be done, just as we feel an increase of self-respect when we obey the law of justice, of integrity within us.

A famous artist said he would never allow himself to look at an inferior drawing or painting, to do anything that was low or demoralizing, lest familiarity with it should taint his own ideal and thus be communicated to his brush.

There is everything in holding a high ideal of your work. Hold the idea of excellence constantly in your mind, for whatever model the mind holds, the life copies. What we think, that we become. Never allow yourself for an instant to harbor the thought of deficiency, inferiority.

Reach to the highest, cling to it. Take no chances with anything that is inferior. Whatever your vocation, let quality be your life-slogan.

Many excuse poor, slipshod work on the plea of lack of time. But in the ordinary situations of life there is plenty of time to do everything as it ought to be done, and if we form the habit of excellence, of doing everything to a finish, our lives would be infinitely more satisfactory, more complete; there would be a wholeness instead of the incompleteness that characterizes most lives.

There is an indescribable superiority added to the very character and fibre of the man who always and everywhere puts quality into his work. There is a sense of wholeness, of satisfaction, of happiness, in his life, which is never felt by the man who does not do his level best every time. He is not haunted by the ghosts or tail ends of half-finished tasks, of skipped problems; is not kept awake by a troubled conscience.

When we are trying with all our might to do our level best, our whole nature improves. Everything looks up when we struggle up; everything looks down when we are going downhill. Aspiration lifts the life; groveling lowers it. When we are striving for excellence in everything we do the entire life grows, improves, but when our standards are dropping, there is a downward tendency in the whole nature.

It is never a merely optional question whether you do a thing right or not, whether you half do it or do it to a finish, there is an eternal principle involved, which, if you violate, you pay the penalty in deterioration, in the lowering of your standards, in the loss of self-respect, in diminished efficiency, a dwarfed nature, a stunted, unsuccessful life.

Don't think you will never hear from a half-finished job, a neglected or botched piece of work. It will never die. It will bob up farther along in your career at the most unexpected moments, in the most embarrassing situations. It will be sure to mortify you when you least expect it. Like Banquo's ghost, it will arise at the most unexpected moments to mar your happiness. A single broken thread in a web of cloth is traced back to the girl who neglected her work in the factory, and the amount of damage is deducted from her wages. Your botched jobs, your neglected tasks will mortify you years hence and keep you from the success you expected.

On every hand we see men seriously embarrassed by the ghosts of skipped problems and neglected faults, sins of omission committed at school or at work, way back in their youth.

Thousands of people are held back all their lives and obliged to accept inferior positions because they cannot entirely overcome the handicap of slipshod habits formed early in life, habits of inaccuracy, of slovenliness, of skipping difficult problems in school, of slurring their work, shirking, or half doing it.

These skipped points in business or in life, the half-finished jobs, the problems passed over in school because they were too hard, are sure to return later in life and give endless trouble and mortification.

Neglecting or half doing things is as if a general in war time should go through a country with an army, leaving here and there a fortress untaken, and pushing on, only to find later the enemies in these uncaptured fortresses firing on his army and harassing him continually.

Half doing things "just for now," expecting to finish them later, has ruined many a bright prospect, because it has led to the habit of slighting one's work. "Oh, that's good enough, what's the use of being so awfully particular?" has been the beginning of a lifelong handicap in many a career.

I was much impressed by this motto, which I saw recently in a great establishment, "WHERE ONLY THE BEST IS GOOD ENOUGH." What a life-motto this would be! How it would revolutionize civilization if everyone were to adopt it and use it; to resolve that, whatever they did, only the best they could do would be good enough, would satisfy them!

Adopt it as yours. Hang it up in your bedroom, in your office or place of business, put it into your pocketbook, weave it into the texture of everything you do, and your life-work will be what everyone's should be—*a masterpiece.*

As Cosimo's mission is to inform and inspire audiences
around the world by offering unique titles, here are
additional titles by Orison Swett Marden

Please visit our website for our latest list of titles: **cosimobooks.com**

BE INSPIRED, BE INFORMED

COSIMO is a specialty publisher of books and publications that inspire, inform, and engage readers. Our mission is to offer unique books to niche audiences around the world.

COSIMO BOOKS publishes books and publications for innovative authors, nonprofit organizations, and businesses. **COSIMO BOOKS** specializes in bringing books back into print, publishing new books quickly and effectively, and making these publications available to readers around the world.

COSIMO CLASSICS offers a collection of distinctive titles by the great authors and thinkers throughout the ages. At **COSIMO CLASSICS** timeless works find new life as affordable books, covering a variety of subjects including: Business, Economics, History, Personal Development, Philosophy, Religion & Spirituality, and much more!

COSIMO REPORTS publishes public reports that affect your world, from global trends to the economy, and from health to geopolitics.